Owls sleep all day and hunt at night.
They have big eyes and can see in the
dark. They catch mice with their long
claws. Owls make nests in hollow trees.

1   Is the owl a big bird?
2   What colour are his feathers?
3   What helps the owl to see?
4   Can owls see well in the dark?
5   Where does the owl build his nest?
6   What colour are the owl's eggs?
7   How does the owl catch his food?
8   What do owls eat?
9   What does the owl do at night?
10 Does the owl live near a town?

Gulls

herring gulls

There are many kinds of gulls. Some live
by the sea, others live in parks, in fields
and along river banks. Many gulls live
together and they are always looking for food.

1 Do you see gulls near to your home?
2 What kinds of gulls can you see in the pictures?
3 Where has the seagull built his nest?
4 How many eggs are in the nest on the cliff?
5 Do you think the nest is in a safe place?
6 What is the seagull diving to the water for?
7 Who is feeding the gulls by the river?

black headed gulls

TOWER BRIDGE

THAMES LASS

black headed gulls

8   What are the gulls looking for in the fields?
9   Which gulls are following the plough?
10   Are gulls big birds?
11   Why are the gulls staying near to the fishing boats?
12   Do gulls live by themselves?
13   Are gulls hungry birds?
14   What will the gull's long wings help him to do?

herring gulls

Blue tits

Blue tits are small garden birds. They often nest in a hole or in a nesting box. Blue tits have large families and are friendly birds.

1 Are blue tits big birds?
2 What are the blue tits eating out of the bag?
3 What is on a string for the birds?
4 What has the man made for the blue tits?
5 Why do birds come to people's gardens?
6 Where do blue tits like to nest?

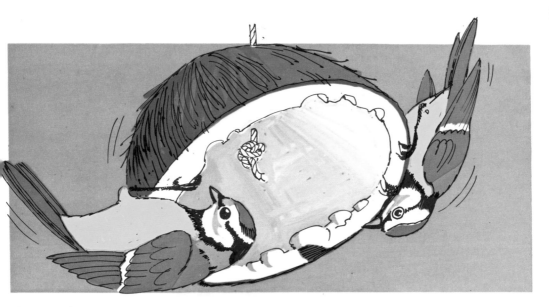

7 Do blue tits like coconut?
8 Why has the blue tit pecked a hole in the milk bottle top?
9 Can all birds hang upside down?
10 What do blue tits like to eat?
11 Do blue tits lay a lot of eggs?
12 Is the blue tit's beak a long one?
13 Do blue tits like cheese?
14 What colours can you see on the blue tit's feathers?

Pigeons

Pigeons are tame birds. A lot of them
live in towns. They are noisy birds and
make a mess on buildings. Farmers do not
like pigeons because they eat the crops
he has grown.

1 Where do a lot of pigeons live?
2 Are pigeons friendly birds?
3 What are the people giving the pigeons to eat?
4 What colour are pigeons?
5 What do pigeons do to buildings?
6 Where has the town pigeon built his nest?

7   Are pigeons noisy birds?
8   Where have the field pigeons built their nests?
9   How many nests can you see in the field?
10 Do pigeons eat wheat and berries?
11 Why do farmers not like pigeons?
12 Why has the farmer put a scarecrow in his field?

Ducks and Swans

Ducks eat bread, worms, small fish and insects. At night they fly to fields to eat grain when it is ripe. Swans eat small frogs, fish, bread and insects. Ducks and swans have webbed feet which help them to swim.

1 Are the ducks and swans hungry?
2 How many ducklings can you see?
3 Are the ducks as big as the swans?
4 What are the people feeding to the ducks?
5 What do ducks and swans dive for?
6 What colour are the ducks?
7 Why do ducks and swans have webbed feet?

8   Where is the duck's nest?

9   What colour are the swans?

10   Is the cygnet the same colour as the swans?

11   Why do ducks sometimes fly to fields at night?

12   What do swans eat?

13   Can the swans fly?

14   What colour are the duck's eggs?

The Heron

The heron is a tall bird with long legs. He builds his nest in a tree. The nest is made with sticks and the eggs are pale green. Herons live near water.

1   Where do herons live?
2   What is the heron on the bank eating?
3   Do herons eat frogs?
4   Why does the heron need long legs?
5   Where does the heron walk to look for food?
6   What colour is the heron?
7   Where does the heron build his nest?
8   What is a heron's nest made with?
9   Are the heron's feet webbed?
10   What colour are the heron's eggs?

Birds in Flight

barn owl

duck

gull

swallow

pigeon

pheasant

1 Do birds look just the same when they are flying?
2 Do all birds have the same shape of tail?
3 What has man made which is shaped like a bird?
4 Which of these birds do you think is fastest
   in flight?
5 Do gulls fly about more than owls?

Farmyard Birds

hens

Hens lay eggs which we eat. Chickens, ducks
and turkeys are bred for food. Some people
like to eat a turkey or a goose at Christmas
time.

1 How many kinds of birds can you see on the farm?
2 What is the farmer collecting from the hens?
3 Are all the hens the same colour?
4 Which birds are bred for food?
5 What will the farmer do to the turkeys at
   Christmas time?
6 Are the hens as big as the turkeys?

turkeys

7   Do you think hens and turkeys are good at
    flying in the sky?
8   What is the farmer's wife doing?
9   Can all the birds in the picture be eaten?

geese

ducks

10   What is under the hen sitting on the nest?
11   When eggs hatch, what comes out of the shell?
12   Why do birds sit on eggs?

chicken

turkey

Looking at Birds

1 Are all birds the same size?
2 How many legs do birds have?
3 Do birds like people to go very near to them?
4 Are all birds covered with feathers?
5 Are all birds the same shape?
6 Do all birds have wings?
7 Which of these birds has the shortest legs?
8 Which of these birds has the longest neck?

9 Which bird has the longest tail?
10 Which bird has big webbed feet?
11 Which of these birds is the smallest?
12 Which of these birds has the longest legs?
13 Which of these birds has a red breast?
14 Do you think birds are interesting to watch?
15 Which bird do you think is the most beautiful?
16 Why is it kind to feed birds in winter?

Pheasant and Grouse

grouse

pheasant

Some birds are called game birds because men
hunt and shoot them for sport. Pheasants eat
the farmer's grain crops, berries and insects.
The grouse is a bird of the hills. He eats
heather, berries and leaves.

1   What are the men holding in their hands?
2   What will the men do with the birds after they
    have killed them?
3   Who brings the dead birds back to the men?
4   Why are some birds called game birds?
5   Is the pheasant a friend of the farmer?
6   Where do grouse live?
7   What do grouse eat?
8   Which of these two birds has the longest tail?
9   Where have the grouse built their nest?
10   Is the grouse as colourful as the pheasant?